COMING TO GRIPS WITH
YOUR ROLE
IN THE
WORKPLACE

COMING TO GRIPS WITH YOUR ROLE IN THE WORKPLACE

ERWIN W. LUTZER

MOODY PRESS

CHICAGO

© 1992 by
ERWIN W. LUTZER

All Scripture quotations, unless noted otherwise, are from the *New American Standard Bible,* © 1960, 1962, 1963, 1968, 1971, 1972, 1973, 1975, and 1977 by The Lockman Foundation, and are used by permission.

ISBN 0-8024-3586-6

1 3 5 7 9 10 8 6 4 2

Printed in the United States of America

Coming to Grips with

YOUR ROLE IN THE WORKPLACE

When I'm at home I'm one person. When I am at work I'm another," Del said, complaining about the pressures that his job put upon him.

"When I'm with Christians I act like them; at work nobody even knows that I'm a church-goer, much less a born again believer."

Del was working seventy hours a week trying to please a demanding boss who expected ever more from his employees. To quit meant that he would be without a job in a competitive market. To continue meant that he was cheating his family and jeopardizing his health.

His wife's critical attitude toward his long hours of low paying work drained whatever romance was left from their relationship. Now he was tempted to seek fulfillment with a woman who adored him, a woman whose friendship would be free of the tensions that existed in his home. He began to consider an affair with this woman co-worker.

Del knew that with his job dilemmas there were no easy answers, perhaps no answers at all. To quit after two years of training and heavy time investments was unthinkable; to continue was to be pulled even further away from his family. Now even sexual temptation lurked on the job. He was convinced that there were no reasonable options.

What should he do?

As Americans earning a living in the late twentieth century, we face a set of challenges unknown to previous generations. With the proliferation of knowledge and inventions, we are told that there are perhaps 50,000 different kinds of possible jobs, demanding a wide range of training and aptitude. Many of these responsibilities are highly specialized and require years of training. Finding the one that best matches our abilities, temperament, and pocketbooks is indeed a difficult task.

Millions of jobs also demand intense interpersonal relationships that spark conflict and force individuals to make decisions with unclear ethical guidelines. Whereas previous generations faced rather simple day by day responsibilities, our technological and informational explosion has created a whole new set of problems. Stacks of books on such topics as tension, managing conflict, and workaholism testify to the pressures of the workplace.

If you are dissatisfied with your career, you have plenty of company. Even as early as 1976, researchers in New Jersey reported that up to 80 percent of Americans are in the wrong jobs![1]

Nevertheless, the pressure-packed working world is a great place for personal and spiritual growth. In fact, *the complex demands of the twentieth century workplace form the best laboratory to prove the reality of God.* Right in the midst of corporate America, with its evercrumbling ethical structure, is one of the best opportunities to prove that Christ can make a difference.

The purpose of this booklet is to challenge Christians to bring God from the sidelines to the very center of the workplace. *Your Role in the Workplace* is a wake-up call to hear the voice of Christ telling us that every single day on the job is a day of eternal significance.

Specifically, this booklet will show that:

- Christians in the workplace are strategically placed there by God.
- Most of the biblical heroes were not in full-time ministry but had regular jobs that they shared with the unbelieving world of their day.
- The ethical pressures of the marketplace are tests given to us by God to let us prove that our love for Him is stronger than life itself.
- God often uses our dislike of a particular job to teach us lessons we could never otherwise learn.
- To "let our light shine" in the workplace means that we have earned the right to be heard.

Our vocations are an entrance exam to see where we should be slotted in the coming kingdom. Christ told several different parables, each emphasizing the same point: those who are faithful with what God has given them will receive a reward in heaven; the careless will suffer loss. Not everyone who enters heaven will hear, "Well done, good and faithful slave; you were faithful with a few things, I will put you in charge of many things; enter into the joy of your master" (Matthew 25:23).

The purpose of the judgment seat of Christ is not to berate us but that we might be assigned a responsibility that corresponds to our degree of faithfulness, including our diligence at work. All believers will be fulfilled in the kingdom but some will have more responsibility than others.

Is God interested in your work? It may come as a surprise that God Himself is a worker. After creation we read, "And by the seventh day God completed His work which He had done; and He rested on the seventh day from all His work which He had done" (Genesis 2:2). God created the world and it is described as work. He upholds creation and that is work. Because we are created in the image of God, we also were created to be workers.

CREATED TO WORK

Most of us suspect that work came about as a result of the curse. In truth, God intended that we work. Even before Adam and Eve sinned we read, "And the Lord God planted a garden toward the east, in Eden; and there He placed the man whom He had formed. Then the Lord God took the man and put him into the garden of Eden to cultivate it and keep it" (Genesis 2:8,15). Sin makes work harder, but by no means was it the cause of work.

We were created to work; indeed work is man's lot by virtue of the design of God. Through work we affirm our partnership with God in governing the world. Ecclesiastes 3:13 teaches that work is a gift of God.

Tragically, with few exceptions, God has been shut out of the workplace. The chasm between Sunday and Monday seems too wide to span. Keen observers tell us that very little that happens in a person's religious life profoundly affects his job.

The Princeton Religion Research Center found "little difference in the ethical views and behavior of the churched and the unchurched" in a recent study of the impact of religion on day-to-day work. Comparing "churched" workers with those workers who do not regularly attend church, the Princeton center surveyed a wide range of behaviors, such as pilfering supplies (stealing), overstating qualifications on résumés (lying), calling in sick when not sick (lying and cheating), and overstating tax deductions (lying, stealing, and cheating). The center concluded that any differences are of marginal significance.[2]

FULL-TIME CHRISTIAN WORK

Often we speak about ministers and missionaries as being in "full-time Christian work." This simply means that some people are paid for using their specialized gifts of ministry full time. Unfortunately this terminology often perpetuates the mistaken idea that these people are serving the Lord more "fully" than those in a "secular" vocation. Some Christians in the workplace see themselves as second-class citizens in the kingdom, not truly serving God. As a result, they don't even seriously consider the scope of their opportunity to serve God. They confine His demands upon their lives to one day a week.

Call to mind the person whom you consider to be most devoted to doing the will of God. If you are like most Christians, you probably thought of a missionary or pastor. Although such are exercising their special gifts of God, many people in other vocations are equally faithful and having just as great a spiritual impact.

What does the Bible teach about the role of believers in the workplace? And what is the divine perspective on work? Christ answers that question by demonstrating the compatibility of a vocation and spiritual ministry.

CHRIST IN THE WORKPLACE

When Christ came to His hometown, Nazareth, the people were astonished that He could teach with such wisdom. They asked, "Where did this man get these things, and what

11

is this wisdom given to Him, and such miracles as these performed by His hands? Is not this the carpenter, the son of Mary and brother of James, and Joses, and Judas, and Simon? And are not His sisters here with us?" Mark adds, "And they took offense at Him" (Mark 6:2, 3).

Not this teaching from a carpenter! Christ offended them because He did not follow the expected cultural pattern. He was not a full-time religious worker and yet He was doing spiritual ministry.

He is neither a scribe nor a Pharisee and yet had the nerve to perform "religious" duties! they thought. *How can this common carpenter speak for God? A man with splinters in his hands and callouses should stay in the pew where he belongs! Full-time carpenters are not supposed to teach in a synagogue. They don't know God well enough to do miracles.*

Apparently they were not offended by what Christ said, but by His occupation. "Is not this the carpenter, the son of Mary?" And they wonder what right He had to teach. *He is the son of a common laborer. Spiritual leaders do not arise out of secular professions.*[3]

Yet here, for all time, Christ demonstrated both the dignity of work (in His case being a carpenter) and the compatibility of such vocations with spiritual ministry.

12

What about the other spiritual leaders of the Bible? Were they full-time religious workers, or did they also have "secular" vocations?

Pete Hammond has done a study of forty leading characters of the Bible, the people who are held up to us as examples of spiritual commitment. He calls these people "Surprising Saints" because of the conclusions he reached in his study (Hammond presented his findings in a message at The Cove, Asheville, North Carolina, on June 29, 1985).

Of these forty leading characters, Hammond discovered three out of every four (75 percent) never had a religious job. They didn't leave the business world to go into "full-time ministry." They held what we call secular jobs all of their lives. Whether it be Joseph, David, Luke, or Paul, they all had their own professions and never did leave these responsibilities so that they could "really" serve the Lord.

If they lived today, they would possibly be treated as second-class citizens, spiritually speaking. With the false dichotomy between those who are in full-time service and those who aren't, they would be told, "All that you can do is pray and pay."

Recently I visited an Islamic country that will not allow missionaries within its borders. At a conference, I met more than 120 believers from the United States and Europe wholly committed to sharing the gospel as witnesses for Christ in this hostile culture. Every one of them had his own job: computer operators, English teachers, businessmen, writers, etc. Clearly they are as important to the kingdom as full-time pastors and missionaries.

In fact, these people told me that their vocations gave them an authenticity that they could not have if they had been allowed to be full-time missionaries. After all, if Christ is credible, He must be proved to be so in the very fabric of everyday life. The pressures of the workplace give Christians the greatest opportunity to prove the authenticity of the gospel.

To make the light shine in a religious gathering is easy enough. However, God wants our lights to shine much farther—in hospitals, the courts, government, schools, factories, and the offices scattered throughout the land. Light must shine in darkness.

The distinction between the clergy and laity is understandable (I myself belong to the first group), but it has led to the crippling impression that those who are in secular vocations cannot serve Christ as fully as those who have chosen religious careers.

In addition, ten of those forty Bible characters had prison records, Hammond notes. Joseph, Daniel, Jeremiah, Christ, Peter, Paul, and others had been incarcerated for one reason or another. Today such people (with few exceptions) would likely never be welcomed by the average evangelical church.

We might also add that many of those whom God used had a past blot on their lives that needed the forgiveness and restoration of God. Moses was guilty of manslaughter, David committed adultery, and Paul the apostle had spent his preconversion days rounding up Christians and having them thrown into jail. Thankfully, God still uses imperfect people today. One of my friends says, "Have you ever noticed how often God puts His hand on the wrong man!"

How many vocations are mentioned in the Bible? Hammond counted eighty-six different jobs among those forty people. Apparently the idea that only the priests were really servants of God did not occur to them. They wrestled with virtually all the pressures that dominate the marketplace today: unreasonable demands from a superior, competition, unfairness, prejudice, job insecurity, and being fired.

Hammond says that for the faith of a believer to be trapped into one day a week (Sunday) is an embarrassment to the work of God. Clearly you can do the will of God without leaving the marketplace. Christ must be Lord not just on Sunday but from Monday through Saturday too.

The church will not have a significant impact on the world until there is a revival among the laity. Only when believers everywhere are willing to see their vocations through the eyes of Christ (whatever the cost) will the authenticity of the gospel make its mark in our society.

Regardless of your vocation, someone has faced the same pressures as you and has done so successfully. Someone has used the struggles and temptations you face to prove the reality of Christ. Our task is to see that the God who ordained that man should work is available to use every believer in almost every vocation as a powerful witness for His glory.

ETHICS IN THE WORKPLACE

Whether on Wall Street, Capitol Hill, or in Christian ministries, our ethical standards have eroded. As I write, one television network news show has just shown a documentary on how service stations pad their bills and how small investors lost their money in a "scam." On another station, a video clip tells how a public school principal told her teachers to help students cheat on test scores so that the school (and her leadership) would look good. Meanwhile the hidden lifestyles of religious leaders are being exposed to a cynical world. Quite literally we have to ask whether anyone can still be trusted.

We can't insulate ourselves from participating (at least in some way) in the ethical dilemmas of our fallen world. I have a friend who will not go to a restaurant that has a bar, believing that patronizing such an establishment supports the liquor industry. I can respect his conscience, but no amount of separation will keep us from becoming a part (at least indirectly) of the evil network within the world's system. I may buy a car that was assembled by employees who will use their incomes for drinking and immorality. I pay taxes to a government that will squander its resources on destructive social legislation and overpriced defense technology. Like it or not, we are a part of the fabric of this fallen society.

Paul told the Christians in Corinth not to associate with someone who claimed to be a believer but lived an immoral or dishonest life.

But he affirmed that such associations are necessary with people of the world. "I wrote you in my letter not to associate with immoral people; I did not at all mean with the immoral people of this world, or with the covetous and swindlers, or with idolaters; for then you would have to go out of the world. For what have I to do with judging outsiders? Do not you judge those who are within the church? But those who are outside, God judges" (1 Corinthians 5:9, 10; 12-13).

How should Christians relate to this sinful environment? To live and work in an immoral world without compromising our convictions is the challenge that every working person faces. How do we remain ethical in a competitive, unethical workplace?

PERSONAL HONESTY

One day while shopping in Hong Kong, I visited an electronics shop owned by a Christian man. We got into a discussion about the widespread "price gouging" that took place in virtually all the stores along his busy street. Then, in a candid moment he surprised me by saying, "I cannot operate this business and be totally honest. If I wouldn't play at least some of the games of the trade,

I'd be out of business because of the competition."

I was struck both by his honesty (to me, if not to all of his customers) and the evident pressure he felt to remain competitive. He didn't exactly enjoy being dishonest, but he thought he must be in order to survive.

Is dishonesty excusable if it is necessary for economic survival? I told this man (though too feebly, I fear) that God had confronted him with a wonderful opportunity. He was given a clear mandate to see whether God was trustworthy or not; here was a well-defined trial that could either prove God or disprove Him.

What if he were to run his business honestly and entrust the success or failure of it wholly to God? And if it failed, would not his obedience be even more precious in the sight of God? Are there not times in all of our lives when we prove that our relationship with God means more to us than life itself?

George Mueller, who founded several orphanages in England in the last century, said that the care of children was the secondary purpose of these ministries. His first objective, he said, was to prove that God was trustworthy. Businessmen were compromising their principles for economic survival. They would not believe Mueller when he asserted that God could take care of them if only they would trust in His promises. So he began these orphanages determined he would never ask for funds but trust wholly in God for daily support. One miracle after another was documented as God provided food and money, often just in the nick of time. We desperately need people today who develop our confidence in the trustworthiness of God.

Not everyone is called of God to begin orphanages by faith. But we are all called upon to be honest, even in the face of economic disaster. How else can we show our fundamental belief that God is trustworthy and can take care of His children? The Almighty does not need our dishonesty to keep food on our table; He meets the needs of those who trust Him in other ways. Dishonesty is always proof of distrust.

Stuart Briscoe tells the story of how he was expected to be dishonest when he worked for a bank in England. He replied to his boss, "If you expect me to steal *for* you, what makes you think that I will not eventually steal *from* you?" Whether the boss appreciated his honesty or not, Briscoe said no when asked to violate his conscience. And it was God's responsibility to take care of the consequences.

We must also remember that dishonesty is more than simply stealing money from the cash register. Theft can take many forms. Workers may steal time by taking extra long lunch breaks or making personal telephone calls at the company's expense. In these and a dozen other ways, dishonesty cuts into the very lifeblood of the business world. Again the Scriptures are clear, "Let him who steals steal no longer; but rather let him labor, performing with his own hands what is good, in order that he may have something to share with him who has need" (Ephesians 4:28).

In those gray areas where we are not sure whether complete honesty is required, we can follow this simple rule: I will treat others the way I would like to be treated if I were in their shoes.

What about the negative fallout a commitment to honesty might have? Remember Shadrach, Meshach, and Abednego? They refused to compromise their commitment to God even at the pain of death. When told that they would be thrown into the fiery furnace, they affirmed their faith that they would be delivered, but added that even if God did not deliver them, they would never worship a false god (Daniel 3:17-18).

As Christ's witnesses we should be willing to do what is right whether the earthly outcome is positive or negative. Honesty does not have to pay in this life to make it worthwhile; it will bring a windfall in the life to come.

To first-century Christians who faced severe persecution for their faith, Peter said that suffering for Christ should not be thought of as strange. The apostle wrote, "Beloved, do not be surprised at the fiery ordeal among you, which comes upon you for your testing as though some strange thing were happening to you; but to the degree that you share the sufferings of Christ, keep on rejoicing; so that also at the revelation of His glory, you may rejoice with exultation. If you are reviled for the name of Christ, you are blessed, because the Spirit of glory and of God rests upon you. By no means let any of you suffer as a murderer, or thief, or evildoer, or a troublesome meddler; but if anyone suffers as a Christian, let him not feel ashamed, but in that name let him glorify God" (1 Peter 4:12-16).

Peter says the world is largely hostile. But our enduring such persecution is precious to Christ. In our endurance we are believing that in the end Christ will have proved Himself totally trustworthy.

When Judge Clarence Thomas faced Anita Hill on national television during Senate hearings to confirm him to the Supreme Court, the issue of sexual harassment sailed into the public eye. Recently, a celebrated court case in Texas raised the question of whether freedom of speech gives men the right to make sexual innuendoes in the presence of women.

For the Christian the answer is clear. "Do not let immorality or any impurity or greed even be named among you, as is proper among saints; and there must be no filthiness and silly talk or coarse jesting, which are not fitting, but rather giving of thanks. And do not participate in the unfruitful deeds of darkness, but instead even expose them" (Ephesians 5:3-4, 11).

Sexual temptations, both to harass and seduce, will exist whenever men and women are in the same environment. But there can be no compromise for Christ's followers, either in speech or actions. Immorality is the surest way for a Christian to ruin his or her witness, and it can destroy an entire family at the same time.

One day a man confided to me that he was falling in love with a co-worker and had a strong feeling that they would soon be having an affair. I told him that he should quit his job.

"But," he protested, "I have a wife and children to support." He apparently didn't realize that if he acted out his fantasies he would have brought more harm to his family than resigning from his job could ever have done! Better to live in poverty and be acceptable to God than commit immorality and incur the displeasure of the Almighty (Hebrews 13:4).

Again, I must stress that honesty and sexual fidelity don't always pay immediately. When Joseph said no to the sexual advances of Potiphar's wife, she lied about him and he was thrown into prison. So much for the notion that serving God is always a sure route to vocational advancement. But the God who was with Joseph in his promotion was now with him in his demotion, too. Eventually, God turned it around for good (see Genesis 39: 20-23; 41: 38-44).

Thousands of believers have been fired because they will not accept the unethical practices of their boss or company. Others have had to voluntarily resign, having to choose between God and their jobs. An employee of a company that specializes in pornography put it this way, "When I finally made Christ Lord of my life, I decided it would be better to go hungry than to work for a firm dedicated to promoting what God hates."

Remember, when we suffer injustice because we have sought to do good, we are especially pleasing to God. Servants, Peter says, should be submissive to their masters, even if those masters are unreasonable. Then he continues, "For this finds favor, if for the sake of conscience toward God a man bears up under sorrows when suffering unjustly. For what credit is there if, when you sin and are harshly treated, you endure it with patience? But if when you do what is right and suffer for it you patiently endure it, this finds favor with God" (1 Peter 2: 19-20). To suffer unjustly attracts the favor of the Almighty.

Earning a living is very important, but is it more important than obedience to God? If obedience cost Christ His life, should we be surprised when the obedience of one of His followers costs him a job?

FINANCIAL FAIRNESS

If you are giving your best to your boss and to the company, you would expect to be compensated fairly. But the word *fairness* sometimes means one thing to employees and another to management.

The book of James has some very pointed words for managers or employers who cheat their workers; it also has some words for those who are the victims of unfair compensation.

As for those employers who exploit the poor, James says that they should weep and howl for the miseries that will surely come upon them. The gold and silver they stored up would actually be evidence held against them in the day of judgment. Then he continues, "Behold, the pay of the laborers who mowed your fields, and which has been withheld by you, cries out against you; and the outcry of those who did the harvesting has reached the ears of the Lord of Sabaoth" (James 5:4).

Imagine working in the fields all day making your boss rich and yet not being paid! Employers can be smug about their selfish misuse of their employees because they think that no one will ever even the score. They forget that every transaction they make will eventually be meticulously reviewed by the Judge of all the earth.

I've even known Christians who were unfair to their employees by underpaying them and making unreasonable demands. If such employers are doing well financially because of the exploitation of others, they have a covetous heart. This too shall be revealed in the last day.

What does James say the poor should do about this unfairness? Obviously they could not appeal to a labor relations board. In those days they had no court of appeal, no grievance committee that would listen to their outcry. But there was one thing they could remember which would satisfy their desire for justice. "Be patient, therefore, brethren, until the coming of the Lord. Behold the farmer waits for the precious produce of the soil, being patient about it, until it gets the early and the latter rains. You too be patient; strengthen your hearts, for the coming of the Lord is at hand. Do not complain, brethren, against one another, that yourselves may not be judged; behold, the Judge is standing right at the door" (5:7-9).

God, he says, monitors all business transactions and in the end will personally address all of the injustices that have ever taken place in employer-employee relationships. Obviously, the oppressed should do all they reasonably can to get what is their due. But the painful fact back then as now is that many of these grievances will never be rectified in this life. But rectified they will be by a Higher Court.

Of course today we can use every legitimate avenue to make our complaint known. But if we reach an impasse we must realize that injustices are used by God to test our faith. Do we believe that we eventually will be adequately recompensed for our faithfulness despite the unscrupulous actions of our employer? Can we not only receive good from the hand of God, but also adversity? Can we put our complaint before the Lord and leave it there? And, can we trust God to meet our needs in other ways?

To the man or woman who has been defrauded of money that is his due, James assures us that the cry for justice has reached the ears of the Lord of Hosts. During this waiting period the wronged person should turn his grievance wholly over to God. Once that transfer of responsibility is made, the oppressed can rest assured that God will do right. And God will walk with the person through it all.

SOUND SPEECH

Our words on Monday, not what we sing on Sunday, best reveal our hearts. Christ said, "The good man out of his good treasure brings forth what is good; and the evil man out of his evil treasure brings forth what is evil. And I say to you, that every careless word that men shall speak, they shall render account for it in the day of judgment. For by your words you shall be justified, and by your words you shall be condemned" (Matthew 12:35-37).

Here perhaps more than anywhere else, a Christian can gain the credibility that is so important in communicating the Christian faith. Three rules must be followed to assure wholesome conversation in the workplace.

First, we must steadfastly *refuse to join in critical gossip* even if the person spoken about deserves all the unkind things said about him. Second, *speak positively about everyone*, even those who may be cruel and demanding. Jesus taught that if we love only those who are lovable, we are no better than the world. Only when we love our enemies are we "God-like" (Luke 6:32-35). Third, *share criticism only with those who are either a part of the problem or part of the solution.*

James reminds us, "And the tongue is a fire, the very world of iniquity; the tongue is set among our members as that which defiles the entire body, and sets on fire the course of our life, and is set on fire by hell. But no one can tame the tongue; it is a restless evil and full of deadly poison" (3:6, 8).

If "tongue control" seems impossible, let us remind ourselves that the Holy Spirit indwells us so that we might be able to control the uncontrollable. Our speech will soon reveal the extent of our commitment to the God whom we claim to love and serve.

We cannot control our circumstances, but we can control our reaction to them. To contain our anger, to speak words that help rather than hurt, is a distinguishing mark of Christian conduct. Against the backdrop of our depressing crisis in ethics, Christians have the opportunity of displaying the character of Christ. Such conduct will attract the attention of the world.

YOUR ATTITUDE IN THE WORKPLACE

Ideally, each person should match his or her abilities with the right vocation. Each of us was made by God with a unique combination of aptitudes and gifts that cry for expression. You may desire to be a teacher, while your brother wants to be an attorney or in medicine. Many workers are content with common labor or one of the many helping professions. Books have been written to help us find a job we can love. I have a vocation that fits my gifts and temperament; I know many others who do not.

What if it doesn't happen, and you now work at a job you don't enjoy?

If being a Christian cannot transform our attitude toward a job we dislike, then the promises of the New Testament are largely empty and

30

Christ's credibility is tarnished. If the reality of God is best proved in the workplace, it must be proved also in the life of a Christian who has a job he or she dislikes.

The painful fact is that many people simply never find the right job/gift mix. Multitudes—perhaps the majority of the work force—dislike what they are doing. But the need for money forces them into jobs that ignite frustration, boredom, and ethical conflict. Many play a state lottery hoping that hitting the jackpot will extricate them from the daily grind they endure but don't enjoy.

Good news is available: If we yield ourselves to God and see our work from His perspective, we can have our attitude changed so that we can find fulfillment even in a job we don't enjoy. Or to put it differently, we can find a source of satisfaction that comes from a world that exists beyond the daily grind.

Christ Himself was given a painful assignment when He stepped out of eternity into time at Bethlehem, an assignment that was far from enjoyable in human terms. His job description was infinitely beneath His dignity: an itinerant evangelist without a home, delivering a message that was rejected by the religious establishment.

He began in the glories of heaven, sharing the same nature and grandeur as His heavenly Father. From there He went to the humiliation of being unrecognized among His own creation. He accepted insults without reminding anyone that He had the power to crush them with a word from His mouth. He began higher and ended lower than any of us could possibly imagine.

Consider the irony: "For by Him all things were created, both in the heavens and on earth, visible and invisible, whether thrones or dominions or rulers or authorities—all things have been created by Him and for Him" (Colossians 1:16). Yet Christ chooses to wash His disciples' feet. He who created their feet now stoops to wash them!

We chafe at the thought of being asked to do something beneath our dignity. Imagine a Ph. D. in mathematics consigned to teach second grade arithmetic; or the president of General Motors asked to manage a hot dog stand.

DOING GOD'S WILL

What was the secret of Christ's being able to adapt to His assignment? He had the confidence that He was doing the will of God. "For I have come down from heaven, not to do My own will, but the will of Him who sent Me" (John 6:38). Before He left heaven, He knew that His daily assignments had been meticulously organized. He would teach, perform miracles, and eventually die at the young age of thirty-three. This ignominious end would purchase salvation for the people whom the Father had given Him.

Most of us think that obedience was easy for Christ. But His divine nature was united with a human nature subject to all the emotional and spiritual stresses that we face. On the human level Christ was not doing what He pleased. The cross and all that led up to it was tough and painful. He learned obedience by these things that He suffered (Hebrews 5:8). The will of God was not a path of uninterrupted tranquility.

One fact sustained Him: *Heaven would make up for the pain of earth*. So He served with one eye on the Father, always mindful that no circumstance on earth could counterbalance the ultimate bliss of obedience: ". . . who for the joy set before Him, endured the cross, despising the shame, and has sat down at the right hand of the throne of God" (Hebrews 12:2).

Christ endured because He knew that it's not what you do but who you do it for that makes the difference.

This perspective worked for Christ, but is it realistic? Could we actually serve that way? Could we actually work for Him as He worked for His Father?

BEING A SERVANT

Put yourself in a time machine and go back 2,000 years and imagine that you are one of 60 million slaves in the Roman Empire. You don't have any recognizable rights. (Aristotle said, "A slave is a tool with a soul.") There are no opportunities for you to choose a vocation in line with your gifts and aptitudes. You have no chance for a promotion and, if abused, you have no court of appeal. This, humanly speaking, is simply the card you have been dealt.

When Paul wrote to these Christian slaves he said, "Slaves, be obedient to those who are your masters according to the flesh, with fear and trembling, in the sincerity of your heart, as to Christ; not by way of eyeservice, as men-pleasers, but as slaves of Christ, doing the will of God from the heart. With good will render service, as to the Lord, and not to men" (Ephesians 6:5-7).

Paul has often been criticized for supposedly condoning slavery. Some prefer that he would have agitated for organized rebellion among the slaves so that they could have been freed. Instead, he says in effect, "Be a good slave."

Paul was not insensitive to their plight. He addresses the masters also, urging them to be kind and reasonable (v.9). He fought slavery through the only way available to him, namely, by the preaching of the gospel. This would transform both slave and master so that there might be mutual respect and equality. As the years progressed, Christianity was the force that eventually brought an end to slavery in the civilized world.

Thankfully, slavery, at least in the Western world, does not exist today. No employer has the right to treat his employees as slaves; workers do not *have to* work for any employer, business, or company. Yet despite the cultural changes, Paul gives three revolutionary principles that remain valid in the workplace today. His teaching will help all of us change our attitude in the workplace as we serve Christ.

1. Don't work for men, but for Christ. Just as Christ served the Father, Paul taught that the slaves should in turn serve Christ. They should switch masters without changing jobs. They were to see their master as the one whom Christ had personally assigned to them. They were to be obedient "as to Christ; not by way of eye-service, as men-pleasers, but as slaves of Christ."

As every manager knows, there is a big difference between a man-pleaser and someone who serves with single-mindedness. Eye-service means that a person works only when the boss is looking. Think of all the eye-service that goes on in today's marketplace, where work breaks are needed to offset coffee breaks.

Second, they were to serve in "fear and trembling," knowing about their accountability to God. Millions today work with the fear of being harassed, fear of being humiliated by an irate boss, and fear of being fired. But to "fear Christ" means that we are aware of our personal accountability to Him.

Would we cheat Christ by taking extended coffee breaks? Would we tell a lie to Christ to make ourselves look good? Would we demean Him to others? I think not. Paul told the slaves that they should treat their master as if he were Christ.

But what if he was mean and unfair? Again, in the absence of any court of appeal, Paul says that Christian slaves should remember that the sufferings of this present life are but a sliver of time in light of eternity (see principle #3, page 40). Any one of us could put up with a mean slave owner if we knew that within six months we would receive a large inheritance and live in uninterrupted bliss. A reward awaits the faithful; a reward that will last infinitely longer than any abuse on earth. Can we believe God like that?

To Titus Paul wrote that slaves were to be subject to their own masters, to be "well pleasing, not argumentative, not pilfering, but showing all good faith that they may adorn the doctrine of God our Savior in every respect" (Titus 2:9-10). To serve their master well would make the gospel attractive to all who cared to notice. This should be the priority of every worker.

2. Don't work for advancement but for fulfillment. Among the slaves were those who had special gifts for drama, music, and the various trades. Some, if they had had an opportunity, would have been great writers and artists. But few, if any, of these people would ever have the opportunity of fulfilling those dreams.

Work can bring wonderful fulfillment to our lives. The craftsman, the attorney, the writer—all of us know the exhilaration of having completed a project, doing our best! But the slaves in Paul's day were locked into their routine without vocational freedom. Yet Paul exhorted them to consider themselves as slaves of Christ "doing the will of

God from the heart" (v. 6). Though they would never know vocational fulfillment, they would have a sense of spiritual fulfillment, serving Christ even though their work was arranged for them by their masters.

What happens if we don't get that promotion? What happens when we work hard and someone else gets the credit? What happens when we don't get to do the very thing we think we were born to do? Is fulfillment dependent on our finding the right job?

Unfortunately, many people think it is. In our culture so much of who we are as individuals is determined by our vocation. Our achievements are often the ticket to acceptance and a healthy self-image. We want to achieve something so that the world will notice. The man who is a failure at home will be tempted to spend extra hours in the office where he is perceived as being a success. Workaholism is often a refuge from having to face the reality of failed relationships. It is a sign of insecurity.

How different it would be if we saw our vocation as an opportunity to "do the will of God from the heart." We would be much better equipped to handle the disappointments in the workplace. Our identity would not be as closely tied to our promotions, achievements, and salary. We would not sacrifice our family on the altar of success; we would accept every day as a gift from God, the blessings and the blahs.

I have yet to meet a person who was fired from a job who believed that he/she deserved it. Like a child in a house of mirrors, most of us spend much of our time finding a mirror that will make us look good. I do not minimize the pain, anger, and sense of loss that comes with a pink slip of dismissal. But if we can accept our demotions as well as promotions as God's will, then the harsh reality of the workplace can be made bearable.

Our identity as a child of God remains secure no matter what happens in our vocations. Our relationship with Him can do what a promotion cannot; it can make us see a silver lining even in swirling, unpredictable clouds.

The bottom line: what does God think? Ask yourself, "Have I served Him to the best of my ability? The opinions of others, though important, cannot make me a victim of the workplace. I refuse to have my dignity made dependent on the evaluation of men whose opinions will not be asked for at the judgment seat."

There is a legend that when Christ was on earth he asked each of His disciples to pick up a stone and carry it. After a few days, He turned these stones into bread. The he asked each disciple to pick up another stone, and each chose a larger one. They carried their burdens for many days without any instructions. Finally they came to a river. Then Christ told them, "Throw your stones into the water." They looked at each other in astonishment, wondering what their hard work had accomplished. But Christ answered, "Why do you wonder? . . . For whom do you carry the stones?"

If you have to carry stones at work, carry them for Christ. No matter what the task, if Christ gives you a job, it has value.

If you have a boring, routine job in a factory, let every turn of the wheel be done for Christ. If your boss asks you to do the lesser task, do it for Christ. "And whatever you do in word or deed, do all in the name of the Lord Jesus, giving thanks through Him to God the Father" (Colossians 3:17).

3. Don't work for time but for eternity. Paul again encourages the slaves by reminding them that whatever good each one does, "this he will receive back from the Lord" (Ephesians 6:8). Eternity puts time in perspective.

Maybe you have seen a truck stacked with flattened cars on their way to the recycling shop. At one time somebody actually had borrowed money to buy one of them; somebody actually became irate when the first dent occurred on the vehicle. But all that doesn't matter now. If time can put the past in a different perspective, think of what eternity will do.

"Since all of these things are to be destroyed in this way, what sort of people ought you to be in holy conduct and godliness, looking for and hastening the coming of the day of God, on account of which the heavens will be destroyed by burning, and the elements will melt with intense heat" (2 Peter 3:11-12).

All that will be left from our hard work is the approval we receive from Christ for having served Him. The people whose lives we touched, the attitude with which we accomplished the routine, the love we demonstrated —only these things will survive the flames.

God is generous. He will overcompensate the losses our faithfulness cost us on earth. But only those who serve with the right motivation will hear the commendation "well done."

Three kneeling men were asked what they were doing. The first said that he was chiseling stones; the second said that he was earning a living; and, a third said that he was building a cathedral. It's all a matter of perspective.

41

I've known Christians who have quit their jobs because there were no other Christians in their firm or office. Apparently they did not realize that they had been planted there by God for the express purpose of being Christ's exclusive representative. Such a person should no more leave because of a lack of Christian influence than a missionary should quit serving in a culture hostile to the gospel. Both are equally called to let their "lights shine."

What gives you as a Christian the right to be heard in the workplace? In a word, it is *credibility*. Christians can easily turn their candle into a smudge pot by having a witness that is forced, hypocritical, or "super-saintly." We've all met believers who make us feel uncomfortable because of their sanctimonious piety that reeks of crafted dishonesty. They leave tracts lying around, they squelch laughter and in general make their religious commitment obnoxious. They think that they would be betraying Christ if they were to admit to personal faults, so they appear to lack genuine understanding of the problems of others.

How can one have a clear witness for Christ that is credible? Peter's presciption still stands: "Sanctify Christ as Lord in your hearts, always being ready to make a defense to every one who asks you to give an account for the hope that is in you, yet with gentleness and reverence" (1 Peter 3:15).

Witnessing must be done with humility, an attitude that respects others even if they belong to a false religion or no religion at all. Nothing turns people off more quickly than someone who believes that because he has the truth (and Christians do) he has the right to disparage others. Given the skepticism that exists about Christianity, we must win a hearing among unbelievers.

Second, a credible witness is one who can give reasons for the hope within himself. Many helpful books have been written about the rationality of the Christian faith. Those who are serious about their witness will become students of the historical and logical underpinnings of the Christian faith.

Third, Peter says that we should respond to people who "ask us to give a defense" for the hope that is within us. Obviously, we have the responsibility of initiating a discussion of the good news of the gospel. But if we are living for Christ, those who are seeking (namely the spiritually hungry) will *ask* us why we are different. God provides those opportunities for His people who look for them.

In about 1850 a group of explorers came across a significant amount of gold in a riverbed in Montana. But they were so weary that they decided they would return home, regroup, get better tools, and after a few days return for the gold. They made a pact, promising each other that they would not share the news with anyone so that they could get the gold for themselves.

Yet, incredibly, when they left early one morning to return to the riverbed, fifty of the townspeople followed them. Had someone shared their secret? When they asked for an explanation, they were told, "We knew that you had found gold by the smiles that were on your faces."

Do our colleagues know that we have found gold? If Christ has made us different, others should be attracted to our source of peace and joy. The change within should show without.

Christ has appointed you to represent Him right where you are. You are the best witness many people will ever meet.

GOD IN YOUR WORKPLACE

Elisabeth Elliot, missionary and author, said that she spent one year working on the details of an obscure language in South America. One day a suitcase with all of the word studies, dictionary, and phonetic structure was stolen. Though many prayed that it would be found, it never was.

Was she bitter because a whole year's work was to no avail? No, anger at God had never occurred to her. "After all," she said, "that year of work was a sacrifice to God, and that could never be lost."

That kind of sacrifice is proof that we actually do believe in God, that we do believe in eternity, and that service to the Almighty will have its rewards in His time.

C.S. Lewis wrote, "The work of a Beethoven and the work of a charwoman become spiritual on precisely the same condition, that of being offered to God, of being done humbly 'as to the Lord.' This does not, of course, mean that it is for anyone a mere toss-up whether he should sweep rooms or compose symphonies. A mole must dig to the glory of God and a cock must crow.⁴"

How specifically can we begin to take eternity seriously? How can we offer a sacrifice to God that will prove that we can live for heaven here on earth? Though it will take some dedication, we can prove to a skeptical world that God can be believed.

Here are some practical steps to bring God into your workplace:

1. *Surrender yourself and your talents wholly to God.* This transfer of your life should be specific, complete, and repeated every single day.

45

2. *Begin a program of Scripture reading* (including memorizing verses) that will cause you to focus on God and His promises every morning. The object is to see every one of your responsibilities as coming not from your earthly boss but from Christ Himself. See your duties as an opportunity to "serve Christ from the heart."

3. *Ask God to show you hidden compromises you have made in the workplace.* Ask God for wisdom to begin making the right decisions, no matter the cost. If you are afraid to trust Him, do it anyway in an act of prayerful surrender.

4. *Commit yourself to one other Christian for regular prayer and accountability.* Promise to live in your home and in the workplace as if Christ were returning to earth next week.

5. *Pray daily for every one of your co-workers by name.* Trust God to give you opportunities to witness to the salvation Christ died to give to those who believe.

Only that which passes the test of death is worthy to pass the test of life. When God is central in our work we will be successful in those things that really matter.

Notes

1. Doug Sherman and William Hendricks, *Your Work Matters to God* (Colorado Springs: Navpress, 1988), p. 131.

2. William Hendricks, "What's Wrong with This Picture?" *Christianity Today,* November 25, 1991, p. 12.

3. These insights about Christ's vocation as a carpenter are based on Peter Hammond's study. I am indebted to Hammond for this material, presented at The Cove conference center on June 29, 1985.

4. C.S. Lewis, *The Weight of Glory* (Grand Rapids: Eerdmans, 1947), pp. 48-9.

Moody Press, a ministry of the Moody Bible Institute, is designed for education, evangelization, and edification. If we may assist you in knowing more about Christ and the Christian life, please write us without obligation: Moody Press, c/o MLM, Chicago, Illinois 60610.

Books in the Salt and Light series: